Items should be returned to the library from which they were borrowed on or before the date stamped above, unless a renewal has been granted.

LM6. 108. 5

Wiltshire
COUNTY COUNCIL

EDUCATION & LIBRARIES

BYTHESEA ROAD

TROWBRIDGE

♺ 100% recycled paper

The Best Reptile Pets

Jerry G. Walls

T.F.H. Publications, Inc.
One TFH Plaza
Third and Union Avenues
Neptune City, NJ 07753

This book has been published with the intent to provide accurate and authoritative information in regard to the subject matter within. While every precaution has been taken in preparation of this book, the publisher and author assume no responsibility for errors or omissions. Neither is any liability assumed for damages resulting from the use of the information herein.

ISBN 0-7938-3109-1

Printed and bound in the United States of America

Printed and Distributed by T.F.H. Publications, Inc.
Neptune City, NJ

Contents

What Makes a Good Pet Reptile?

S cientists called herpetologists have been describing new reptiles since 1758, and after almost 250 years they have recognized the existence of about 7,900 distinct species. These are distributed as follows: 2,900 snakes; 4,650 lizards and amphisbaenians; 300 turtles; and 25 crocodilians and tuataras, with the number growing by about 60 species each year into the near future. (For full details, see Uetz, 2000, *Herpetological Review*, 31[1].) Yet of this quite respectable number, probably only some 400 to 500 species are regularly available for terrarium hobbyists to keep as pets. Why are most reptiles unsuitable for the home terrarium? Or perhaps a better question would be, why are 500 species keepable in the terrarium?

Few reptiles have been able to make the transition from nature to the terrarium, and the species that are commonly kept as pets are exceptional in many ways. They generally are relatively sedentary animals that will accept confinement in a glass or plastic cage of 50 gallons (190 L) or less, having little interest in continually trying to force their way through transparent walls or screened lids. (Many snakes and lizards have large home ranges in nature and never adapt to being confined.) They are animals that for some reason are able to get used to human presence and overcome a natural instinct to flee or bite when handled. In no case do good pet reptiles have specialized diets that hobbyists would find difficult or impossible to duplicate in the home. Undoubtedly there are many snakes, for instance, that would make excellent pets if only they did not have to be fed on lizards or frogs their entire lives. Hobbyists want pets that will thrive on a diet of mice or crickets, with occasional treats and supplements.

A good pet reptile is adaptable to temperatures and humidity ranges found in average households, being able to thrive with minimal heating, a light for basking, and occasional mistings to control humidity levels. If they need extremely narrow temperature ranges (stenotherms), they seldom survive in the home, where temperatures may vary by more than 40 degrees F over a single day. Likewise, they have to be able to survive in the dry heat used in most American and European households, as most hobbyists find it too expensive and time-consuming to install and maintain complicated equipment to more closely control the temperature and humidity.

If a reptile can breed successfully in captivity without the use of hormones or complicated schemes varying the light, temperature, and humidity to resemble those of its home area, so much the better. For the past decade there has been a growing movement to recommend only captive-bred reptiles as pets. This is a natural outcome of excessive commercial taking of many species, not just reptiles, for food, skins, medicines, and pets, along with a great loss of natural habitats around the world. There is little information on the number of individuals of each reptile species in nature, but certainly some that are commonly kept as pets are no longer as commonly found as they were 50 or even 25 years ago. By emphasizing species that can be bred in captivity in numbers large enough to satisfy a commercial market, new imports become unnecessary and there is one less threat to natural populations of reptiles. Of the 15 basic recommended species in this book, at least 12 are easy to find as true captive-bred young specimens, including all the snakes and lizards. In the years to come, different species probably will become more common as captive-breds and either supplement or replace some of the species on our list, but this is only to be expected and hoped for.

This "banana" phase California Kingsnake, Lampropeltis getula californiae, *is an excellent example of careful selection of captive-bred specimens.*

Although Madagascan Ground Geckos, Paroedura pictus, *are easily kept and bred, their dull colors probably will keep them from ever becoming wildly popular.*

Of course, no matter how adaptable a reptile species may be, if it is dully colored or extremely secretive it is not likely to become a popular pet. Though many specialist terrarium keepers look upon their charges as a challenge and are more interested in them as ways to expand their knowledge and skills, the beginning reptile keeper generally cannot be challenged too much. The beginner wants a pet that can be handled, thrives even with occasional mistakes on the part of the keeper, and, admittedly, can be shown off to friends on occasion. A reptile that must stay hidden under deep layers of moss or sand to be comfortable, one that virtually never is visible on the surface of the terrarium, is not a fun animal to own and seldom makes it big in the commercial pet market. Regardless of changing attitudes about the relationships of humans and their pets, it is still a fact that most keepers are owners first and observers second—a pet is kept, at least at first, for pride of ownership; only with increasing experience do many hobbyists realize that a snake or lizard has many lessons to teach them and that the human—pet relationship is really a form of symbiosis.

In this book we'll take a look at 15 basic terrarium reptile species, all of which have shown themselves to be adaptable to the very unnatural conditions in the terrarium and keepable by patient beginners with minimal equipment and expense. Almost all of these are readily purchased as young specimens that have been carefully bred in captivity by dedicated commercial or hobbyist breeders. These captive-breds carry few parasites, are in good health, come from carefully planned matings, and often have greatly intensified or modified colors compared to wild specimens. They are unstressed and are used to readily available cultured foods that you can find in any pet shop or grow at home. These are among the best of all pets if your inclinations are toward the cool-blooded, scaly sort.

You will notice that the listing of best turtles is much more tentative than that for snakes and lizards. There are fewer than 300 turtle species to choose from to begin with, and of these perhaps half are uncommon or rare in nature and virtually unavailable. The resulting small number of possible pet species has made it difficult for turtles to become established as really good pets for beginning keepers, and almost all turtles actually are not keepable as easily as many snakes and lizards. All pet turtles have problems regarding their keeping conditions, temperature and light schedules, and feeding requirements, and it would be hypocritical to say that any turtle really makes a good pet for a beginner. Few are bred commercially in captivity. The species discussed later are the best of what are now keepable by dedicated hobbyists willing to make some concessions to their pets. Keeping turtles requires much more effort and often expense than keeping other reptile pets. Additionally, several areas have passed laws restricting ownership of turtles of many common species and in some cases all species. These local laws must be obeyed for both the good of the turtles and the future of the hobby. If your area does not allow the keeping of, for instance, box turtles, don't illegally keep those species. Find a more suitable and legal substitute. Most restrictive laws on keeping turtles have a real basis in fact, as turtles seldom live long or reproduce in captivity and often are in serious trouble in nature, with reduced numbers of individuals in the wild due to over-collecting, losses on highways, and destruction of natural habitats.

The listing of best reptiles is of course not exhaustive, and in many ways it represents the favorites of the author, just as any "best of" list will have a bias. For this reason I've included mentions of a few other similar species or groups with some of the favored species. These secondary

Some of the most beautiful snakes, such as this "high red" Honduran Milksnake, Lampropeltis triangulum hondurensis, *require care beyond the abilities of many casual keepers.*

Rhacodactylus ciliatus, *the Crested Giant Gecko, has gone from endangered species to readily available in just a few years and may eventually become a viable choice for beginners.*

species are "almost as good" as the principal ones but perhaps are a bit larger or more nervous or are harder to feed or house. They also make excellent pets, but for various reasons they are not quite as easy to keep and cannot be given quite as high of a recommendation.

I've also included a short chapter on reptiles that—in my opinion—are best not kept by beginning or casual reptile hobbyists. Some of the animals mentioned are obvious, such as venomous species, but others may go against the grain of what you see offered in any pet shop. Remember that just because a species is sold everywhere and at low prices does not mean it makes a good pet. In fact, it often means just the opposite—the cheapest reptiles often are wild-collected and horribly stressed adults of species that just cannot adapt to the terrarium. Other commonly sold reptiles are babies of species that grow much too large for the average household.

Over the years my wife and I have kept almost all the animals mentioned here and most of the secondary species as well. We have seen the reptiles available to hobbyists improve in quality and variety, as well as longevity and ease of keeping, and expect to see the hobby continue to improve year to year. Amazingly, few of the 15 best species discussed here have been widely available for more than a decade, so you can see that the reptile hobby is still in its infancy. The best is certainly yet to come.

The Best Snakes

S nakes make fascinating pets, and there is a wide variety of species available, from the slender, semiaquatic garter snakes (*Thamnophis*) of North America to pythons that often exceed 20 feet (6 meters) in length. There certainly are 100 species that regularly reach the commercial market, many available in a variety of colors and subspecies, but of this number it seems that fewer than 20 to 30 species dominate the hobby. The most popular snake species are captive-bred in small to large numbers each year by a variety of commercial and hobbyist breeders, and they are easily available and generally inexpensive for their high quality.

For the beginning terrarium keeper, snakes offer a wider variety of excellent species than do the lizards, which still are heavily dependent on imported, wild-caught specimens of most species. The following five species are my choices for the "best" pet snakes suitable for the beginner or casual hobbyist. They include:

1) Corn Snake
2) Ball Python
3) Common Kingsnake
4) Rosy Boa
5) Western Hog-nosed Snake.

In almost every case, there are several very similar species that are nearly as good in the terrarium as my major selections. More detailed information on all these species is available in a variety of books and magazine articles, and all the species are very well-known in the terrarium.

One: Corn Snake (*Elaphe guttata*)

Also known by the "book name" Red Rat Snake, the Corn Snake is undoubtedly the most familiar pet snake today. A relatively slender species with a small head, the Corn Snake is native to the southeastern United States, ranging from New Jersey to Louisiana, with a similar but more dully colored species (the Great Plains Rat Snake, *Elaphe emoryi*) found west of the Mississippi River to Utah and northern Mexico. Few adults are much over 3 feet (0.9 meters) in length, though old females may be 4 to over 5 feet (1.2 to over 1.5 meters) long. Young specimens are very slender, but the species does bulk up as it matures, with older females often having a distinctly thick body compared to the small head and slender neck. In nature this species is grayish tan to bright orange-tan above, glossy white below, with a series of more or less squarish bright red-brown spots outlined in black running down the center of the back; many specimens are studies in pink and orange. The first spot (on the nape) has two arms at its front edge that run forward over the top of the head and then join in a spearhead-shaped point. The belly has many large black squares, these tending to form two regular stripes under the tail. As in other rat snakes (genus *Elaphe*), the scales down the center of the back are keeled (with a raised ridge down the center of each scale), but the contrasting colors of most specimens give them a relatively glossy appearance.

Corn Snakes have been bred in large numbers for more than a decade, and today they are sold in literally dozens of colors and patterns. The most common commercial variety probably is the albino (amelanistic), in which the dark brown/black pigments are missing. This results in the red and yellow colors appearing intensified. Albinos vary greatly in appearance, with the best being bright pink with scarlet markings on the back. Albinism is an easily inherited genetic trait that can be introduced into lines of other varieties to produce distinctive colors. For instance, in some Corn Snakes there is a tendency for the spots on the back to send out lines that fuse with the corners of the neighboring spots. Breeders have developed this tendency into a strongly striped pattern. When albinism is added to the genetically striped Corn Snake lineages, a gorgeous snake with red stripes on a pinkish background is produced. Other colorful varieties include blood red Corns, where the red pigment is greatly intensified so some adults may be uniformly bright red; anerythristics or black albinos, in which the dark pigments are present but the red pigments are absent; and Snow Corns, produced by a cross between an albino and an anerythristic, so neither red nor black pigments are present, resulting in a solid glossy white snake. Normal or wild-type patterns also are produced by breeders in a diversity of tones and color intensities, with the most contrastingly colored specimens often being called Okeetee Corns after a classic collecting locality. Many minor and relatively inconstant color varieties also are bred, and several new color varieties are marketed every year. At any large reptile show you are bound to see examples of a dozen or more such varieties; making a selection often is difficult because there are just so many pretty Corn Snakes available.

If possible, try to choose a Corn Snake about a year old as your first pet. Such a snake is almost certain to be healthy and has had many meals, so it is used to the small mice that form the major part of the diet. A Corn Snake may live 8 to 12 years, sometimes longer, so by starting with a young snake you are certain to get almost a decade of enjoyment from your new pet. If you purchase a hatchling, one only a month or two out of the egg, you face the possibility of sudden unexplained deaths in these babies (rare but not really unheard of) and the possibility that they may not feed well. A Corn Snake is mature at between 18 and 24 months of age (males maturing earlier than females, as usual for snakes). As a rule, males are a bit shorter than females and have proportionately longer, more gradually tapered tails with obvious bulges at the base due to the hemipenes (the snake's sexual organs). Both males and females have similar temperaments and make good pets.

A "flame" Corn Snake, Elaphe guttata, *has a pattern like a wild specimen but has been selectively bred for increased color and contrast.*

Keeping Corn Snakes usually is a breeze, and they are extremely undemanding snakes. An adult (as usual, it is best to keep all snakes individually) can be kept in any type of terrarium, from a simple glass aquarium with a screened lid to an expensive wooden and plastic display terrarium, with a capacity of between 20 and 50 gallons (76 and 190 L). The substrate or bedding can consist of a thick layer of finely shredded aspen, any other good grade of wood shavings—but never cedar, or even just paper towels. A small water bowl, changed regularly, a snug hidebox, and a well-anchored branch positioned just above the bottom of the cage complete the furnishings. Corn Snakes do well at normal room temperatures, typically between 70 and 75F (21 and 24C) during the day, dropping a few degrees at night. They tolerate temperatures into the low 80sF (28 to 30C) well but don't need heaters in most homes. They will use a weak basking light but also don't need one—in nature they are largely nocturnal or at least crepuscular (active at dawn and dusk). Special fluorescent lights also are not needed. In fact, many breeders with large stables of Corn Snakes keep them in simple plastic sweater boxes with no lighting or heating other than that of the room. The usual diet consists of mice, varying from pinkies (just born, hairless) to adults. Both living (pinkies) or freshly killed (adults) and frozen and thawed mice are accepted; many Corn Snakes actually seem to prefer frozen and thawed mice, which don't fight back but are attacked with a full routine of grabbing and constricting before swallowing. Baby Corns usually are fed two to four pinkies a week, while adults may need only a mouse or two every other week. Do not overfeed, as these snakes tend to become obese.

As a rule, if you wish to breed your Corn Snakes (either by buying a specimen of the opposite sex or borrowing or loaning out your pet to a friend with the matching sex) you should cool them a bit during the winter. As with most North American snakes, the sperm mature during the winter, when the snakes would be hibernating in nature. The usual routine is to stop feeding the snakes in mid-November and start letting the temperature gradually drop by about ten degrees below normal, to 60 to 65F (16 to 18C). The snakes are held at this low temperature (often in the dark and always with water available for drinking) for one to two months and then gradually returned to normal temperatures. After a soak or two in tepid water and a meal, often followed by a shedding of the old skin, a male is placed with a female and mating normally ensues almost immediately. Mating is not especially rough in this snake, and the pairs often are left together for several weeks. The female will swell with eggs if gravid and will lay her dozen or so eggs about 60 days after mating, typically a week after a molt. The eggs are incubated on water-saturated vermiculite at 80F (27C) for two months. This pattern of cooling, laying, and incubation is typical of almost all common colubrids (a member of the snake family Colubridae, the "typical" snakes) native to North America and Europe.

Hatchlings are pretty little snakes with especially bright colors. They have their first molt a week to two weeks after emerging and then usually take their first meal. Most Corn Snakes are excellent feeders, but some young may not take their first meal until two or three months of age.

Without doubt, the Corn Snake is the best choice of snake for the true beginner and holds much potential even for the expert keeper. Their colors and ease of care are among the best of the entire

A striped albino Corn Snake bears little resemblance to its wild ancestors. It represents two distinct mutations bred into a single line.

"Candy cane" Corns are highly contrasting albinos. Young specimens are much more colorful than this typical adult.

The "Aztec" Corn is a new and as yet unproved mutation with high contrast and a variably fused and broken pattern distinguishing it from its "normal" ancestors.

group, and they require perhaps the lowest maintenance of any snake. Beautiful specimens are inexpensive, and their terrarium also is cheap to set up. You really can't go wrong with a Corn.

Corn Snakes are just one of several excellent species of *Elaphe*, the genus of common rat snakes, available to hobbyists. Of the other *Elaphe*, perhaps the best is the Yellow Rat, *Elaphe obsoleta quadrivittata*, from the southeastern United States, a form available in a variety of colors. Many *Elaphe* are larger than Corn Snakes and more aggressive. This is especially true of the Asian species such as *E. taeniura*, which recently has been bred in increasingly large numbers.

Two: Ball Python (*Python regius*)

If popularity of snakes were a horse race, the Ball Python would be the dark horse coming up fast on the outside. Just a few years ago, any experienced snake keeper would tell beginners to avoid Ball Pythons at all cost. The imported young specimens found in the shops were weak, stressed, heavily parasitized, and often suffering from respiratory problems. Adults were even worse, often just refusing to eat for months until they used up all stored energy reserves and died. No one ever claimed Ball Pythons were aggressive animals, however, and they have one of the most attractive and distinctive color patterns of all the pythons, but they just could not be kept.

Enter the commercial breeders. In just a few years, Ball Pythons that have been captive-bred locally in the United States, Canada, and Europe have found a ready and appreciative market that will absorb all the young specimens bred each year. Additionally, color varieties now are starting to make an appearance, though still at high prices, and the future looks very bright for this python to become a staple of the terrarium hobby.

Ball Pythons are small by python standards, average adults being some 3 to 4.6 feet (0.9 to 1.4 meters) long, with a few old females reaching as much as 6.6 feet (2 meters) or a bit more. These are much bulkier snakes than any Corn Snake, with the typically small head, short tail, and distinct neck of almost any python. Unlike colubrid snakes, the scales on the back are very small and in over 50 rows around the body and the ventral scales are much smaller than in a Corn Snake; the top of the head is covered with just a few large scales and many small, irregular scales rather than the nine large scales standard in the family Colubridae. Like other pythons, there are claw-like spurs, leg remnants, projecting through the skin on either side of the vent, though hidden under scales and often not easily visible. In males the spurs are distinctly larger than in females; adult males generally are not as long as are females.

Though no two Ball Pythons are identical in details of pattern, the species overall is very constant in its features. The top of the head is dark brown to reddish brown, sharply cut off at the back from the pale golden tan of the nape. A dark brown stripe runs along the upper edge of the lip scales through the eye to the nostrils, isolating a golden tan bar above it. Thus, from the side the head appears dark brown on top, golden, dark brown, and then whitish on the lip scales, the very dark brown to black eye standing out sharply. Down the center of the back is a broad dark brown to reddish brown band with scalloped edges producing narrow dark brown vertical bars. These bars surround horseshoe-shaped golden tan ovals that often have one or two dark brown spots toward their upper edge and may be outlined with yellow. No other regularly available snake is likely to be confused with a Ball Python. Albino, striped, and variously modified patterns now are available.

This is one of the most non-aggressive snakes, though because of its bulk and its membership in the family Pythonidae it should never be treated lightly; a bite from a large specimen definitely hurts. Generally, when touched or gently picked up the snake tries to hide its head under coils of its body. Wild specimens are noted for tightly clenching with the head toward the center of the coils, producing a tight ball that, it has been said, can actually be rolled across smooth terrain. Captives generally remain shy when first picked up but soon find a comfortable position on your arm and may do a bit of casual exploring like any other snake. A Ball Python that is acclimated to handling can even be trusted with a child, if the child is carefully supervised and cautioned to make no sudden movements.

Ball Pythons are a bit more demanding in the terrarium than are Corn Snakes, needing a warmer, more humid terrarium. Start with a 20-gallon (76-L) cage and expect to move to at most a 50-gallon (190-L) for a single adult. Provide a few inches (centimeters) of shredded aspen bedding or equivalent, in which the snake will find a favored spot, over which you can place a suitable hidebox. A large water bowl, changed daily, and perhaps a climbing branch are all you need inside the cage. Above the terrarium place a weak basking light (40 watts usually is suitable) that will warm a small area of the bottom to 95F (35C). Under the terrarium place a heating pad that covers about a third of the bottom and will keep the terrarium at 82 to 85F (28 to 30C). Mist the terrarium daily but don't get the bottom actually wet. The lid of the terrarium must be securely attached as these are strong snakes easily capable of lifting most lids. Because of the need for a basking light and extra heating, Ball Pythons are best not kept in sweater boxes. As usual, specimens are best kept individually.

Ball Pythons, Python regius, *can be among the most beautiful snakes and certainly are the best pythons available for the casual keeper, but true captive-bred specimens are a must.*

In nature Ball Pythons feed on a variety of rodents, and in captivity pets will feed on the usual laboratory mice. They are not heavy eaters and may become obese if fed too often. Almost any Ball Python may go on a hunger strike occasionally for weeks or even a few months, but if healthy and well-fed before, they usually will come out of it without any problems.

Ball Pythons generally do not breed well in household conditions, and they are not easy to breed under any circumstances. However, many breeders do succeed in producing clutches each year, so captive-bred young are always available if you look around. Like other snakes, the pythons are kept a bit cooler (70 to 80F, 21 to 27C) and drier than usual for one or two months during the winter and then put together for mating. Females lay only half a dozen eggs in most clutches, which helps keep the market from being flooded and keeps prices relatively high.

The only caveat with Ball Pythons is that you MUST buy only a specimen that has been captive-bred locally, meaning not in western Africa. Ball Pythons occur widely across central Africa in fields, savannas, and the edges of forests, even in gardens, and still are common. Imported specimens usually have been "ranched" by collecting gravid females, holding them until they lay, and then incubating the eggs. The resulting young are held for sometimes weeks without feeding and then shipped under often crowded conditions. Imported young are among the cheapest of snakes to buy, sometimes even cheaper than Corn Snakes, but they seldom make acceptable pets and should be avoided. You will pay more for a locally (North America or Europe) captive-bred Ball Python, but this can be considered a sort of insurance policy for a good, healthy pet.

Even adult Ball Pythons tend to be shy snakes that are tame when handled gently. They are one of the few snakes that can be trusted with children, if the handling is carefully monitored by an adult.

Normal (black) and hypomelanistic (brown) California Kingsnakes, Lampropeltis getula californiae, *of the ringed variety. In nature, ringed specimens are more widely distributed than striped specimens.*

Three: Common Kingsnake (*Lampropeltis getula*)

One of the most variable snakes in North America, with at least seven subspecies normally recognized, the Common Kingsnake also is one of the few species of snakes actually found from coast to coast in the United States, ranging from New Jersey to California and Oregon and then south into Mexico. These are relatively stout-bodied, very glossy snakes that climb well and have a snout that is shorter and wider than that of a Corn Snake. Few adults are much over 4 feet (1.2 meters) long, but these are powerful constrictors that easily take not only small rodents and birds but also snakes. The common name "kingsnake" itself refers to the snakes being the kings or rulers of other snakes, as they readily attack and kill venomous rattlesnakes and copperheads. In captivity, however, kingsnakes prefer the ease and safety of tackling mice, preferably frozen and thawed first.

Though all the subspecies of *Lampropeltis getula* are kept in captivity and bred in large to small numbers for commercial sale, the most popular subspecies certainly is the California Kingsnake, *Lampropeltis getula californiae*. This chocolate brown to black and white to yellow kingsnake is common in a variety of habitats from southern Arizona west to the Pacific Ocean, being especially prominent in western California. Over most of this range it displays a ringed pattern, but in parts of central California it is striped. Striped populations long were considered to be a full species, *Lampropeltis boylei*, and it was only 70 years ago that direct evidence of the two forms belonging to one species was published. Today the California King is bred in tremendous numbers and in not only the basic ringed and striped phases but also in a variety of patterns and colors from nearly all white to solid chocolate brown. Many keepers prefer patterns that are associated with certain

"Newport Beach" is one of the many striped aberrant varieties of California Kingsnake. These broken-striped snakes are very popular with many keepers.

breeders or localities, but the most common Cal Kings seen today probably belong to a large, amorphous group known as "aberrants." Such snakes commonly are brown with one or several rows of large or small pale spots or blotches, or sometimes with broken stripes. No two aberrants are exactly alike, and there is a pattern to suit almost anyone.

In temperament the Common Kingsnake is fairly friendly and does not mind being gently handled. It often coils firmly around an arm and then begins to search down your shirt front or up a sleeve. Their smooth, shiny scales have a wonderful texture that goes well with their cool bodies. Unfortunately, these kingsnakes are not quite as easy to handle as are Corn Snakes. When first touched to pick one up, they often snap, biting gently but enough to draw blood. These nips can be avoided by very slow movements, never coming on a snake from above, or using a hook to start the lifting. Additionally, some snakes never get over the annoying habit of releasing anal gland contents when handled. This grainy, very smelly substance is smeared over a hand or on clothing, producing a penetrating smell that is strong but somewhat sweet and clinging. Many keepers just get used to the smell, but others find it intolerable. The nipping and the gland secretions probably turn more people off Common Kingsnakes than any other potential problems.

Actually, Common Kingsnakes as pets have few other problems. They can be kept just like Corn Snakes, in a minimally furnished terrarium or sweater box at room temperature with no basking light. Breeding usually occurs after a one- or two-month winter cooling period, a typical female producing a dozen to two dozen eggs. The eggs hatch in eight to ten weeks when incubated on wet vermiculite at 82F (28C). The young take their first meal of pinkie mice soon after their first shed, a week or so after hatching.

Though California Kingsnakes dominate the market of this species, Florida Kingsnakes, *Lampropeltis getula floridana* (native to southern Florida), also are very popular and variable kings. Typical specimens are pale brown with a large cream spot on virtually every scale from head to tail, but there are fascinating blotched and striped specimens from northern and western Florida that represent intergrades with the black and white Eastern Kingsnake or Chain King, *Lampropeltis getula getula*. These odd variants, often called "*goini*" or the Apalachicola King, can be among the most beautiful snakes.

Common Kingsnakes are just one of seven or eight species of *Lampropeltis* found from central Mexico to southern Canada, and all are kept and bred in the hobby. Especially popular are Gray-banded Kingsnakes, *Lampropeltis mexicana alterna*, from southwestern Texas, and the many red-black-yellow-ringed subspecies of the Milksnake, *Lampropeltis triangulum*, found from eastern Canada to the Andes of South America. These species, as a rule, are more expensive than Common Kings and are more difficult to keep and breed, so they typically fall outside the possibilities for the beginning keeper.

Four: Rosy Boa (*Lichanura trivirgata*)

One of the most beautiful and smallest boas (actually burrowing boas, family Erycinidae) is the Rosy Boa, a 2- to 3-foot (0.6- to 0.9-meter), nearly cylindrical, extremely strong, small-headed boa found mostly in southern California and Baja California as well as adjacent Arizona and Sonora.

A classic striped pattern ("Long Canyon") of the Rosy Boa, Lichanura trivirgata. *This little boa is among the most variable of North American snakes, which has led to many color varieties becoming available in the terrarium.*

The top of the head is covered with small scales and the tail is short but distinctly tapered, which helps separate it from its relatives in the genus *Charina* (rubber boas). They are extremely simple in coloration and pattern but totally pleasing snakes that are easy to handle and keep and make great pets.

A typical Rosy Boa (there are many variants) is pale gray, brown, or sandy tan, sometimes almost white or distinctly pinkish, with three broad darker brown (chocolate brown to nearly black) or orange stripes down the back. Some specimens are extremely pale, almost white with very pale orange-tan stripes, while others are entirely suffused with lead-gray. The stripes may be very clean, with straight edges (especially in southern Baja California), or very ragged, giving the back a speckled appearance. Many of these pattern and color variations are restricted to small areas of the total range, and hobbyists often try to get snakes whose parents came from selected areas. Recently, popular locality variants have come from San Felipe (bright orange stripes on a nearly white background) and El Rosario (nearly red stripes on a shiny gray background) in Baja California and Borrego Springs (very jagged stripes and speckling in orange-tan on gray) and the San Bernardino Mountains (highly irregular orange-tan stripes and speckling on a very pale tan, almost white, background) in California. Additionally, breeders have produced very dark specimens (melanistic) and very pale ones (hypomelanistic) with clean, bright markings. As with many captive-bred snakes, there is a pattern to appeal to almost any taste.

Rosy Boas are easy to handle, seldom objecting to being picked up, though they can throw very strong coils around a wrist or finger. The head and mouth are small, even in relation to body length,

An "El Rosario" pattern Rosy Boa. Gentle and easy to keep, brightly patterned specimens of Rosy Boas are very popular and are bred in good numbers.

This cleanly striped Rosy Boa is from northwestern Arizona. If young Rosy Boas were less worrisome to feed, the species would be even more popular than it is today.

and a bite (which seldom happens) is almost painless and seldom even bleeds. When disturbed, the snake often tries to hide its head under its body. These are nocturnal to crepuscular snakes, active during the hours of darkness, which must be remembered when feeding them their small mice. Many specimens learn to accept frozen, thawed mice, but some will always want living pinkies (hairless) or fuzzies (haired but blind or nearly so).

In keeping with their home in the American Southwest, Rosy Boas like relatively warm surroundings. The typical terrarium can be small (10 to 20 gallons, 38 to 76 L), with a deep layer of dry wood mulch or sand at the bottom. A water dish is unnecessary, as these snakes like it dry; offer water once a week in a small dish. Use an undertank heating pad to keep the temperature at 82 to 85F (28 to 30C), dropping slightly at night. Alternatively, a weak basking light (especially a ceramic heat emitter, which produces no visible light) can be kept on during the day to raise the tank temperature above room temperature. Give a snake lots of hiding spots and a hidebox. They seldom climb so don't really need a climbing branch.

Breeding is relatively easy, usually following about three months at lowered temperatures (down to 55F, 13C) with no feeding to duplicate a desert winter. The snakes mate in April, females giving birth to five or six foot-long (0.3-meter) young in September. Unfortunately, young snakes often are difficult to start feeding. In nature they usually are born just before winter sets in, and they do not take their first meal until the following spring, five or six months later. When a young Rosy tries to follow the same course in the terrarium, the keeper naturally gets worried and resorts to all types of remedies, including stressful forced feedings and chemical diet stimulants. Just let the baby stay in a cool, dark spot over the winter and see what happens in the spring—you'll be surprised how often it comes out with a roaring appetite.

Rosy Boas may cost a bit more than the other snakes in the "best" list, but a good captive-bred yearling is well worth the money.

Five: Western Hog-nosed Snake (*Heterodon nasicus*)

There were several good snakes that could have been number five on my list, including Pine and Gopher Snakes (*Pituophis*), garter snakes (*Thamnophis*), and perhaps even Red-tailed Boas (*Boa constrictor*), but at the last minute I decided to give the spot to a relative newcomer, the Western Hog-nosed Snake. This stout-bodied, small-headed, tan and brown-spotted snake is resident in the dry prairies of the central United States, southern Canada, and eastern Mexico. It is a great burrower, with a very compact snout area ending in a pointed, sharp-edged, upturned rostral scale that aids it in digging toads from soft soil. In fact, toads are its main food in the wild, the nocturnal snake finding toads by scent and digging them up; the enlarged rear fangs in the upper jaws are flattened and serve as daggers to slit open an inflated toad and perhaps also inject a very toad-specific venom. Typical adults are 1.5 to 2.5 feet (0.45 to 0.75 meter) long and grayish tan with a series of large dark brown spots (often paired) down the center of the back alternating with two or three rows of smaller spots on the sides. The spots are round to oval and often edged with black. The head pattern is pleasing, consisting of a broad brown band between the eyes and large oval spots behind the eyes and on the nape. Recently a few color variants have been developed, including albinos, but they still are very expensive though likely to drop in price.

Albino and normal juvenile Western Hog-nosed Snakes, Heterodon nasicus. *This hog-nose has proved adaptable in the terrarium and today is being bred in decent numbers.*

Western Hog-noses are one of three species in the genus *Heterodon*, the other two being found widely over the eastern United States (*Heterodon platirhinos*, the Eastern Hog-nose) or restricted to sandy areas in the southeastern U.S. (*Heterodon simus*, the Southern Hog-nose). Of the three species, all of which feed on toads in nature and are noted for a death-feigning display when disturbed, only the Western Hog-nose reliably feeds on mice in captivity. This means that it is the only species suitable for keeping as a pet, certainly at the beginner level. To keep the other species requires keeping a supply of living or frozen toads or scenting mice with toad skin or urine; both these options probably would be considered above and beyond the call of duty by most hobbyists.

In captivity Western Hog-noses are relatively easy to keep, as they need small, simple quarters with a minimum of furniture. One adult can be kept in a 10-gallon (38-L) terrarium with a screened lid and either paper towels or a dry wood mulch substrate such as shredded aspen. The humidity must be kept low, so a water bowl can be left out and presented to the snake just one day a week. Moist surroundings may lead to respiratory ills and possibly death, so keep things dry. (This may make Western Hog-noses difficult to keep in climates that are excessively humid for weeks at a time, something to consider when deciding on a purchase.) Use an undertank heater or a ceramic heat emitter (remember these are largely nocturnal snakes) to keep the cage at about 85F (30C), dropping significantly at night. A hidebox is the only other furnishing needed, as these snakes seldom climb. The snakes are easy to handle, seldom biting though they may strike with closed mouths on occasion. Captive-bred specimens seldom writhe about and fake death as do wild-caught specimens.

Breeding requires a long cooling period, often three months at 55F (13C); keep the holding cage dark and do not feed the snake during this period. Mating takes place about May, so time the end of the cool period for a month or two earlier and feed the breeding pair heavily and keep them warm. Males are told from females by probing for the hemipene pouches; there are no obvious external differences. Females lay a dozen or more eggs that hatch in under two months when incubated at 85F (30C) or a bit less in vermiculite at 75% of saturation. The young may not feed for two or three weeks after hatching.

The Best Lizards

O ver the past decade, lizards seem to have been catching up in popularity with the snakes, but they have many factors going against their further increases in popularity. First, most of the lizards sold today would seem to be Giant Green Iguanas, *Iguana iguana,* plus—at the other end of the size and price scales—the small Green and Brown Anoles (*Anolis carolinensis* and *Anolis sagrei*). Green Iguanas are talked about briefly in the last chapter, where I present a few reasons why they make poor pets for the average hobbyist. Anoles, which often are sold for less than the cost of the simple cages children use to house them, are very active, territorial lizards that need heat, sunlight-equivalent lighting, and a varied diet, plus a surprisingly large cage. They also do not tolerate handling well (a low-point may be having a pet die in your hands while moving it for simple maintenance). Anoles also are almost always wild-caught.

Additionally, few species of inexpensive, moderate-sized lizards are bred in captivity, most lizards sold still being wild-caught. The lizards perhaps most popular with advanced keepers, the monitors (genus *Varanus*), generally are too large and aggressive for beginners, though a few currently very expensive smaller species have great promise for the future. Many of the lizards most easily and cheaply available to hobbyists in the United States are native species collected in great numbers in the late spring and early summer and shipped in truly miserable condition to market, only to die a few weeks later. These desert-dwelling natives, such as swifts (*Sceloporus*) and their relatives, often require high heat and large cages to meet their minimal requirements. Finally, the vast majority of the other lizards often sold in pet shops are relatively unattractive imports about which little is understood of the details of their captive care; this is especially true of the great number of often unidentifiable skinks and agamas sold.

Because this book stresses captive-bred specimens for pets, it has been difficult coming up with even five lizards as recommended species. Some specialists are sure to disagree with my fourth and fifth choices as "best" pets, but at the moment it is hard to think of any lizards that are more accessible, captive-bred, and keepable with relatively few problems. Thus the following are my suggestions of the lizards that should be considered as the "best" pets for beginning and casual keepers:

1) Leopard Gecko
2) Inland Bearded Dragon
3) Blue-tongued skinks
4) Texas Alligator Lizard
5) Green Water Dragon.

One: Leopard Gecko (*Eublepharis macularius*)

Geckos are very specialized lizards that usually have soft, delicate skin that is not covered with overlapping scales but instead appears pebbly. Most species are strongly modified for climbing and have wide adhesive pads under the fingers and toes. In the majority of the geckos, family Gekkonidae, there are no eyelids, the eye being covered by a transparent scale, the brille or spectacle, and the lizard cannot blink. In some 20 species of geckos, however, eyelids still are present; these are the eyelid geckos, family Eublepharidae. Eyelid geckos typically are burrowers in relatively dry habitats, which gives them an advantage in the terrarium. The most familiar eyelid gecko is the Leopard Gecko, certainly the most commonly captive-bred pet lizard in the world today. Leopards are sure to have been noticed by every hobbyist, as they are in almost every pet shop and are sold at low to moderate prices. This is a sturdily built, large-headed terrestrial gecko that seldom climbs and has large, expressive eyes. Adults are some 6 to 8 inches (15 to 20 cm) long, with a few males as much as 10 inches (25 cm) long. The tail is thick and ringed with circles of raised bumps; it is used as an organ of water and fat storage so may be quite swollen in healthy specimens. Though Leopard Geckos will drop the tail if you pull hard enough, this important organ is firmly attached and is more likely to suffer from torn skin than complete loss. Occasionally wild-caught Leopard Geckos are seen with short, badly scarred tails that have been partially regenerated after an attack by a predator in the wild, but captive-bred specimens should have complete, perfect tails. The legs of Leopards are short and slender, with short toes that lack climbing pads. Leopards usually are slow-moving, very deliberate lizards even when young, and they seem to appreciate or at least tolerate gentle handling.

Typical adult Leopard Geckos in the normal or "wild" pattern are tan or yellowish above and white below, covered on the back and sides with numerous large blackish brown spots from the tip of the snout to the tip of the tail. The spots in younger adults may be arranged in vaguely regular bands across the back, a remnant of the hatchling pattern. Juveniles are very different in appearance, being very pale yellow above with three or four broad purple-black bands across the back, a purple-black top of the head (often with large bright blue spots over the eyes where the eye capsules show through translucent skin), and a wide, curved white band on the nape of the neck. The tail in hatchlings is white to pinkish with four broad black bands. The black bands of the hatchling gradually break into the spotted pattern of the adult over the first year or two of the lizard's

The black spots are almost the only remnants of the wild pattern on this adult female "designer" Leopard Gecko, Eublepharis macularius, *carefully bred for color.*

life, so to some extent you can recognize a subadult Leopard by how spotted versus banded it is on the back.

This wild pattern no longer is really typical of the Leopard Geckos sold in pet shops today, because breeders have for years been selecting their breeding stock for a reduction in the black and an increase in the yellow of the pattern. The most highly developed captive-breds, so-called "Hi-Yellows," are brilliant yellow above with little or no dark spotting. In lutinos the brown and black pigments are absent or reduced genetically and the lizard shows an overall translucent yellow coloration. Albinos lack the black and brown pigments but also have the yellow pigment reduced, so the lizard is a translucent white to very pale tan. Lutinos and albinos still are hard to breed and are relatively expensive; in my opinion they are not nearly as colorful as the much more affordable Hi-Yellows. Striped specimens now also are being bred, and it is likely that other unusual variants will become available in the coming years because literally tens of thousands of Leopard Geckos are bred each year.

Keeping Leopard Geckos is easy. Select a captive-bred yearling specimen if possible, one a few months to a year old and still showing remnants of the juvenile pattern. Such specimens are affordable, healthy, and used to handling. Hatchlings, as in any reptile, sometimes die for unknown reasons and may not be the best choice for a single pet, while it is difficult to determine just how old is an adult. (Leopard Geckos commonly live 8 to 12 years.) These sedentary, non-territorial geckos can be kept through their entire lives in a 10-gallon (38-L) glass aquarium, with a 20-gallon (76-L) tank more than large enough for a breeding trio of a male and two

Even t' dark-banded young of Leopard Geckos are more colorful today than in generations past.

females. In their natural range (India and Pakistan and a bit further west) Leopard Geckos burrow in sandy, rocky deserts and plains with sparse vegetation and extremely variable temperatures, from well below freezing during the winter to over 100F (38C) during the summer. Their burrows, however, which may be self-dug or inherited from various rodents, are relatively moist and hold a fairly constant temperature, and this is what you strive to duplicate in the terrarium. Fortunately, captive Leopard Geckos are not strong burrowers, and they do well when given a bottom of deep sand or a sand-vermiculite mix, one corner being kept a bit moist and covered with a piece of curved cork bark as the hiding area. They really need no other furniture, spending much of the day under the bark and coming out at night to slowly walk around the terrarium looking for food. Cover the terrarium with a screened lid so the substrate stays dry and give the geckos a weak fluorescent light that they will use for basking on occasion during the day. They do not need a heat light. In fact, most captive-bred Leopard Geckos do well at warm room temperatures, between 70 and 75F (21 and 24C), with a high extreme of 85F (30C). If you wish, place a small undertank heating pad under the moist corner of the terrarium. Err on the side of cooler temperatures (down to 65F, 18C) rather than warmer ones. A small, shallow water dish will be used for occasional drinking, but lightly misting the terrarium and gecko daily is better. With occasional changing of the substrate and daily cleaning of the cage, your Leopard Gecko will do well here for years. Leopard Geckos also do well in sweater boxes, where they are kept on simple sandy bottoms with a piece of bark and a small water bowl; because they seldom try to escape, they do well in these boxes placed in shelf units without tops, lights, or heat.

Feeding is a breeze, as Leopard Geckos feed well on crickets of appropriate size. Give each gecko two or three crickets in the evening twice a week. Be sure that crickets are not allowed to accumulate in the cage, as they could attack a lizard when they get hungry; provide them with a small dish of greens to ease their appetite. Once a week, when the gecko is likely to be hungriest, coat the crickets with a multivitamin and calcium powder from the pet shop. Gravid females and growing young need more calcium than typical adults. When possible, give the geckos treats in the form of waxworms, small mealworms, or wild-caught small, soft insects to vary the diet a bit. Large adults often will take a pinkie mouse once a month or so. Leopard Geckos seldom go on hunger strikes and are noted as good, consistent feeders. Remember that they are most likely to hunt in the dark, though some pets may be active during the day as well.

It probably is easier to successfully breed Leopard Geckos in captivity than to breed any other lizard. This is why captive-bred specimens have largely replaced wild-caughts and so many different color and pattern varieties are found in the market. Some commercial breeders maintain breeding "herds" of hundreds of trios and produce thousands of young per year. As a rule, Leopard Geckos are sexually mature before the age of two, with some captive-breds laying at less than a year; the loss of the juvenile pattern usually is correlated with the coming of breeding age. Males are longer and more robust than females, with distinctly wider, heavier heads. They also have a row of open pores under the hind legs that secrete a waxy substance that may inform females they are males. To prevent possible problems from competition, two males should not be housed in the same terrarium, but two or three females do well with a single male.

The white and pale yellow coloration of this Leopard represents a mutation often called lutino, perhaps in error. Some breeders now are just calling this a "patternless" Leopard.

Mating takes place at night following little or no obvious courtship, the male chasing down the female, grabbing her nape with his mouth, and twisting her around so he can insert one of his hemipenes. Mating seldom is observed, but a bit over a month after a successful mating the female will be obviously gravid, the two large white eggs being visible through the thin abdominal skin. A gravid female basks more often than usual and needs extra calcium on her crickets. When the eggs become visible, the female is about a week from laying and should be given a plastic sandwich box nearly filled with moist vermiculite as a nesting box; cut a hole of appropriate size in the top or side so the female can enter and leave as she wishes. Females lay two eggs (almost all geckos lay just two eggs in a clutch, but they may produce a clutch every month to six weeks over much of the year) partially buried in the vermiculite, if you are lucky. Some females will just drop their eggs anywhere, and these eggs likely will dry up and die before you find them. Check the laying box twice daily for eggs and keep an eye out for the female suddenly looking slimmer.

Once the eggs are laid, they cannot be turned without risking killing the developing embryo. Carefully mark the upper side of the egg with a soft pencil and then transfer it to a dish of moist vermiculite in an incubator container that holds a constant temperature of 85F (29.5C). In Leopard Geckos sex of the hatchlings is determined by the temperature at certain stages of incubation. As a rule, females develop from eggs held at 80 to 84F (27 to 29C), while males emerge from eggs incubated at 86 to 90F (30 to 32C). These are general rules, with exceptions, but by keeping the incubation temperature at a constant 85F (29.5C) the breeder is assured of a good mix of the sexes over many clutches. Hatching usually takes six to seven weeks, producing the characteristic black-banded 3-inch (7.5-cm) young that are active almost immediately, relying on stored yolk in the intestine for the first week. Like most other geckos, the young usually eat their shed skins (both as a source of nutrition and to remove odorous remains that in nature might attract predators), their first molt being five to eight days after hatching. From that time on they are ready to stalk and eat crickets of appropriate size; crickets should not be longer than the width of the lizard's mouth. Juveniles grow rapidly and need more calcium supplementation than adults if they are to have strong bones and normal skeletons.

Very similar to the Leopard Gecko is the central African Fat-tailed Gecko, *Hemitheconyx caudicinctus*, which at first glance is a bit browner with wider bands on the back than in the Leopard. Fat-tails are a bit stouter than Leopards, males having especially wider heads. They like a bit moister bottom and hiding area than do Leopards, with an overall more humid terrarium that can be a bit warmer on average. Today Fat-tails are being bred in larger numbers than ever and are becoming more common in the shops, with a few color varieties having been developed, including albinos, striped specimens, and yellow replacing the brown. They are a bit more nippy than are Leopards, which almost never bite, and don't seem to tolerate handling as well as do Leopards, but they make truly excellent pets.

Two: Inland Bearded Dragon (*Pogona vitticeps*)

Bearded dragons are about as different from Leopard Geckos as any two lizards can be, yet they have proved to be excellent, attractive pets with thousands of fans. There are several species of bearded dragons on the island continent of Australia, but Australia's laws against exportation of their fauna have meant that only one species, *Pogona vitticeps*, has been widely available to hobbyists for the past 25 years. Found in a variety of relatively dry habitats (from desert to gardens and lawns) of eastern central Australia, the Inland Bearded Dragon bears a strong resemblance to the southwestern North American horned "toads," lizards of the unrelated genus *Phrynosoma*. (*Pogona* belongs to the family Agamidae, *Phrynosoma* to the Iguanidae in the broad sense.) They are large, spiny, flattened lizards with moderately short tails and very wide mouths. A typical adult Inland Bearded (from here on referred to just as the Bearded Dragon or Beardie) is 18 to 20 inches (46 to 50 cm) long, the tail about half this length. The legs are short and strong, with the digits ending in long, sharp claws. The body is depressed (flattened) and covered with large tubercles and soft spines, including two rows of long, pointed spines along the side of the body. The tail and belly are covered with more normal scales. The head is box-like, very deep but wide, with a large eye and short snout. The ear opening is prominent and there are rows of long, sharply pointed spines above and below it and across the back angles of the head. The throat is covered with pointed scales and can be expanded by an angry Beardie into a wide gular pouch edged with long spines and, in males, often black in color. The mouth and tongue are contrasting bright colors, orange to pinkish white, and there are large though rather blunt teeth on the jaws. Make no mistake—an angry Bearded Dragon is capable of a hard, painful bite that can draw blood, and their claws can scratch deeply. Fortunately, they are generally placid lizards that, with the proper care, can be handled easily. The spines, by the way, are not hard structures as you might expect but are flexible and relatively soft (except on the head), so these are not especially prickly lizards to handle.

Inland Bearded Dragons, Pogona vitticeps, *are not especially colorful but are large, generally tame, and bizarrely spiny. In recent years they have become one of the most popular pet lizards.*

Few color varieties of the Inland Bearded Dragon are strongly marked. This "red phase" specimen has distinct tinges of red on the head. Certainly brighter colors will become available in the next few years.

Most Inland Bearded Dragons are sandy brown with narrow pale bands across the back and oval darker brown spots down the center of the back, on each side, and across the tail. There is a dark brown line back from the eye over the jaws, sometimes outlined with white. These basic colors vary greatly from individual to individual and also with temperature and mood. Today there are several relatively indistinct color varieties offered for sale that have increased red tones in the pattern. Known by several names, these red Beardies vary from having barely distinct reddish tones on the head and throat to distinct red tints over the entire body. Tiger Beardies have a broken pattern on the sides, and specimens with increased yellow also are bred. Overall, the color varieties of Beardies available today are expensive and not especially obvious except to the specialist.

Keeping a Beardie requires considerable heating and a basking light as well as a substrate of sand or other dry material with scattered rocks and a sturdy climbing branch or two. Because adults are large lizards, the terrarium should be 40 inches (1 meter) long for an adult, but juveniles commonly are kept in 10- to 20-gallon (38- to 76-L) glass aquaria, which can house three or four young to subadults. Because of weight, cages for adults tend to be made of plastic rather than glass. You probably will not keep more than one adult in a terrarium, as these are territorial lizards even when young, and adult males can inflict serious damage on smaller specimens of either sex. A breeding pair needs a terrarium at least 80 inches (2 meters) long and fairly deep to be comfortable. These lizards like to climb, and this has to be remembered when setting up the terrarium. A small water bowl, supplemented with occasional misting, completes the furnishings.

Beardies like it hot. Start with an undertank heating pad that will bring about half the terrarium to an average temperature of 90F (32C), with the other half staying at 75F (24C) or so, dropping a bit at night. Additionally, a heat emitter or incandescent light bulb in a conical shield over the terrarium (preferably over a favored climbing branch or rock) should produce a local temperature of over 104F (40C) for 12 hours a day. Heaters and basking lights may be expensive to operate and provide fire hazards in some households, something to remember when considering a Bearded Dragon for a pet.

Beardies are omnivores—they eat both plant and animal foods. The basic diet consists of crickets and other insects (the more types the merrier, including adult mealworm beetles and even Japanese beetles and captive-bred roaches) alternated with a salad of chopped greens and root vegetables. Bearded Dragons are not at all choosy about their foods, and they will take almost anything; they have large appetites if being properly kept and warm enough. Commonly crickets (supplemented with vitamin and calcium powder every other week for adults, more often for growing young) are offered twice a week and salads twice a week. Remove uneaten vegetables daily, clean the cage daily, and remove excess insects regularly. Large adults commonly will eat mice, and they also will eat young Bearded Dragons. Remember that these are large, territorial lizards—feeding young from a common dish may result in fights.

Prepared Bearded Dragon foods now are widely available. These usually have a fairly good content of mixed vegetables and fruits, and most Beardies will learn to take them. Some are based on cornmeal and other unsuitable products, however, so be sure to read the ingredient labels careful-

Beardies are aggressive with each other, one of their few faults. Puffing up the throat to reveal the spines and bobbing the head are signs of a dragon with mayhem—or sex—on its mind.

ly. As a rule, Bearded Dragons take insects only when alive and moving, so prepared foods based on dried crickets and similar items may not be accepted by all dragons. Most hobbyists currently seem to prefer to use prepared foods as treats or supplements to a balanced diet of crickets or mealworms and freshly prepared salads. Avoid iceberg lettuce in the salad, by the way; green lettuces such as romaine and endive are much preferred, as are collards, carrots and carrot tops, corn, green beans, kale, mulberry leaves and berries, and even okra. Roses, dandelions, hibiscus, and other brightly colored flowers as well as their leaves often are appreciated as treats. Hatchlings should not be fed mealworms because they sometimes cause a terminal paralysis; both the larvae and adults are fine for larger Beardies, in small numbers.

Inland Bearded Dragons can be bred in the home, though obviously an adult pair will need a large terrarium. Males have larger heads than females, usually have black throats, and have open pores under the hind legs; they are more aggressive than females, often bobbing the head up and down in a characteristic fashion and threatening other Beardies in the vicinity. They breed after coming out of a winter cooling period, when the lizards are maintained separately for three months at temperatures as low as 65F (18C) with just eight or nine hours of light a day and reduced food. Mating itself is rough, and females often are scarred or lose digits. Females lay one to two dozen eggs in a moist burrow about two months after mating. In the terrarium they usually are given a large container (such as a cat litter pan) filled with damp vermiculite in which to dig and lay their eggs. The eggs then are removed (without turning) to an incubator where they are kept at 85F (about 30C) for about two months on a bed of moist vermiculite. As the hatchlings emerge, they

New Guinea Blue-tongued Skinks, Tiliqua gigas, *are widely available and continue to be the most affordable species of the genus. It may take a while to find captive-bred young, however.*

Northern Blue-tongues, Tiliqua scincoides intermedia, *are large, prolific, colorful skinks from dry areas of northern Australia. They also are relatively easy to handle for their size.*

are moved to a 10-gallon (38-L) cage where several can be kept together when heavily fed and carefully watched. They need temperatures and basking lights much like the adults and have about the same diet, of course adjusted for their smaller size (and without mealworms). When several young are kept together, one or more may be picked on by the others and may be attacked, losing limbs and tail.

Though dealers now sell very young Beardies, these probably are not the best way to start with this species. Go instead for a well-grown young specimen at least 6 to 8 inches (15 to 20 cm) long that is feeding well and not missing toes or scarred from juvenile fights. Such a specimen will adapt to handling, and many hand-tamed Beardies enjoy resting on their owner's arm and being gently stroked, even when fully adult. Females remain more gentle than males, but these lizards are difficult to sex until at least a year old. Bearded Dragons have great potential in the hobby if they are not over-bred and especially if new, stronger colors can be developed. With the proper care, they make great pets.

Three: Blue-tongued Skinks

The skinks (family Scincidae) are abundant, secretive, ground-dwelling lizards found through much of the world (though absent from much of Europe), and a variety of small species is imported for the hobby from Africa and Asia. However, the very large (over a foot, 30 cm), short-legged, rather flattened blue-tongued skinks of Australia and New Guinea, genus *Tiliqua*, are the ones that stand out for the beginning hobbyist. These big-headed lizards are noted for the very large bright blue tongue that is flicked on a regular basis and also displayed in an open mouth when the lizard is cornered. Unlike most lizards, these skinks give birth to living young that are much like the adults in appearance, which means that a beginner does not have to worry about setting up an incubator and maintaining it for two or more months.

Two species of *Tiliqua* are widely available as captive-bred specimens in the hobby, though they are not especially inexpensive and may not be easy to find at your local pet shop. The New Guinea Blue-tongue, *Tiliqua gigas*, is found over southern New Guinea and the eastern Indonesian islands. At 20 inches (50 cm) they are big lizards, and they can inflict a painful bite if annoyed, but they generally are fairly calm and can be handled with care. This is not an especially colorful species, being golden brown over the back, white below, with a broad black band on each side that includes the short legs; there usually are black bands across the back. Males may have brighter orange eyes than females, but the sexes are difficult to distinguish. The Common Blue-tongued Skink, *Tiliqua scincoides*, is found over northern and eastern Australia (specimens reportedly from New Guinea are questionably from that island) in generally dry or at least not very humid situations. Two sub-species are present in the hobby and are easily distinguished by color pattern. The Eastern Blue-tongue, *T. s. scincoides*, comes from eastern Australia and tolerates humid conditions best; these 20- to 22-inch (50- to 55-cm) skinks generally are brown above (often bright tan) with darker bands that extend over the sides and angle backward; there is a broad blackish stripe back from the eye. The Northern Blue-tongue, *T. s. intermedia*, comes from drier habitats in northern Australia and is more brightly colored, usually with bright orange ovals on the sides between the dark brown bands coming straight down from the back, the brown back itself being crossed by darker bands that are broadly edged and stippled with white; there typically is no black stripe back from the eye. This is a larger animal than the Eastern, often reaching 25 to 30 inches (63 to 76 cm) in total length. Many hobbyists consider Northern Blue-tongues a great pet, being not only more colorful than the New Guinea or Eastern but also more gentle and easier to handle.

Blue-tongues, because of their large adult size, need large terraria, preferably 40 to 80 inches (1 to 2 meters) long, though young can be kept in 20-gallon (76-L) aquaria. It is best to never keep more than a pair in one cage or there will be fights and possible losses. Even young specimens may be aggressive and should be caged separately. Give them a deep layer of aspen or other hardwood bedding on the bottom of the terrarium, along with several hiding areas such as pieces of curved cork bark. They also need a water bowl (as well as daily misting, especially for the New Guinea Blue-tongue), an undertank heating pad (for the Northern especially), and a basking light. They like temperatures under the basking light of 85 to 95F (30 to 35C) and 75F (24C) in the rest of the terrarium. Many adults do quite well at room temperature without a heater, but the basking light is essential. These lizards often are active during the day and may be very conspicuous when slowly stalking prey or just "hanging out" on a favorite rock. They seldom climb.

As omnivores, blue-tongues take a varied diet of both insects and plants. In captivity it often is suggested that they be given crickets and mealworms once a week and a mixed vegetable and fruit salad once or twice a week. They are especially fond of snails of all types, though these may carry parasites. Specimens that do not feed well on natural foods often will take a good grade of catfood at least once a week; though this in theory should have too much protein for the lizards to remain healthy, in reality many specimens seem to prefer this food and live many years with no obvious signs of metabolic problems. As usual, the key to keeping these lizards is to provide the most varied diet possible. Young specimens grow very rapidly and need large amounts of calcium in the diet if their bones are to be well-formed, so for the first six months or so of life they should be given a calcium supplement with almost every meal. Adults need fewer supplements.

Like many other lizards, blue-tongues breed after coming out from a cool period. They are cooled much like Bearded Dragons and mate in much the same way, with males being especially aggressive. The sexes are almost impossible to distinguish with certainty without checking for hemipenes in the male. There is a great deal of chasing and fighting before mating, and females often are mangled by males, losing toes or entire limbs. The female is placed in her own terrarium after mating and should be fed heavily, given calcium and vitamin supplements, and allowed to bask much of the time. She grows obviously inflated with the young and will be pregnant for four to six months. Most blue-tongues give birth to five to ten colorful, active young, but Northern Blue-tongues may have over two dozen young in a litter. The babies usually are removed to their own terraria within hours of birth just as a precaution and should be kept a bit warmer than the adults for their first six months of life. They will be mature in one to two years.

Because of their sometimes aggressive behavior and need for a large terrarium, blue-tongues may not be for everyone, but they certainly are wonderful pets with a good following. So far few color varieties have been bred, but selective breeding of these lizards is just starting. Who knows what the future holds?

Bright orange ovals on the sides and a fascinating blue tongue combine to make the Northern Blue-tongue one of the most desirable terrarium lizards.

Four: Texas Alligator Lizard (*Gerrhonotus infernalis*)

This selection as a "best" pet may seem a little odd to some people, but I have confidence that a beginner who picks up a nice captive-bred Texas Alligator Lizard will not be disappointed. Note that I said captive-bred; wild specimens are commonly collected for the hobby market, but they cannot be recommended as pets for the casual hobbyist—captive-breds are not difficult to find, are not expensive, and certainly make better pets. This species is one of several alligator lizards (family Anguidae) native to the western U.S., Mexico, and Central America, but it is the only species found in Texas. Part of a group of very similar species ranging from the Big Bend region of southwestern Texas over Mexico, this species was until recently called *Gerrhonotus liocephalus infernalis*, but today it is given full specific rank. It occurs in wooded mountainous terrain from central Texas to the Big Bend and into adjacent Mexico, often being found near springs and rocky streams. Though the area it inhabits is dry, often desert-like, its microhabit is relatively humid and cool, something to remember when designing a terrarium. Adults commonly are 12 to 15 inches (30 to 37.5 cm) long, two-thirds of this a slender, strongly prehensile tail. The body itself is small, with slender but strong legs and a small, tapering head. The scales of the back and sides are keeled, not smooth and glossy as in the skinks, with which alligator lizards often are confused. Young specimens are brightly banded with white and dark glossy brown over the back, but this pattern becomes less distinct with growth until adults are brown with irregular remnants of narrow white bands over the back and brown heads with bright yellow eyes. The body always looks flattened, especially when a cornered lizard inflates the body in an attempt to look larger than it really is. The bite is a strong pinch that seldom draws blood.

These lizards have minimal terrarium requirements. They like it relatively cool and are active both day and (especially) night. One or two specimens (they are not territorial or aggressive with each other) can be housed in a 20-gallon (76-L) aquarium with a screened lid, smaller if you are starting with a juvenile. Cover the bottom with a good grade of hardwood mulch (such as aspen bedding) that holds some moisture. A small water bowl, a few rocks or bits of bark for hiding spots, and several branches for climbing complete the basic furnishings. If you wish, add an undertank heating pad to keep the terrarium at 75F (24C), and provide a weak basking light or a fluorescent light. These lizards dislike stale air and prefer a cage placed outdoors during part of the year and allowing good air movement. During the winter reduce the temperature in the cage to 60F (16C) or so and reduce feeding. Texas Alligator Lizards kept too warm or not allowed to cool during the winter will not stay healthy.

Feeding is simple—crickets, occasionally supplemented with vitamins and calcium, are an acceptable staple. These lizards are famous for their slow-motion stalks of insects, taking several minutes to unnoticeably move up on a cricket before quickly grabbing it. They also hunt while hanging by their flexible tails from branches, grabbing crickets that venture close enough to the unseen arboreal predator. For variety, feed wild-collected caterpillars and small grasshoppers during the summer, or try waxworms. Juveniles need a great deal of calcium in the diet or they will die—they must be supplemented. These are not especially long-lived lizards, but with care a Texas Alligator Lizard may live four or five years in the terrarium.

Slow-moving Texas Alligator Lizards, Gerrhonotus infernalis, *are not colorful but have tons of personality. Keep them cool and be ready to provide calcium and vitamin supplements.*

Breeding is typical of lizards, a male (with prominent hemipene bulges at the base of the tail) finding a female through scent and sight and grabbing her at the nape with his jaws. He curls around her (their long tails making quite a sight) so the vents are opposite and inserts a hemipene. Females, which do not have to be removed to a separate terrarium, become greatly inflated with their eggs and may lay some 10 to 30 eggs in a clutch under a rock or bark on the ground. Unlike most reptiles, the female stays with her eggs, curling about them for the two months they incubate. She must be given a suitably moist nesting box when ready to lay and can be given the occasional cricket while nesting (some females will feed while coiled about the eggs, some will not). After the eggs hatch, the female should be heavily fed to keep her from dying. The young take small insects almost as soon as they hatch and will soon accept handling.

At the moment Texas Alligator Lizards are bred mostly by non-commercial breeders who produce only a few young each year, so they are not always easy to find. However, they are charming, very different lizards noted for their gentle lifestyles and ease of care, and there is something thrilling about watching a Texas Alligator Lizard grabbing a cricket while hanging upside-down from a branch. Other, less slender, alligator lizards from Arizona and the Pacific Northwest sometimes are available, but this species is the only one currently bred in decent numbers in captivity.

Five: Green Water Dragon (*Physignathus cocincinus*)

Green or Chinese Water Dragons are among the most colorful of lizards, even adults usually being bright green with pink and orange tones when warm and healthy. Unlike Green Iguanas, they

Unlike Giant Green Iguanas, adult Green Water Dragons, Physignathus cocincinus, *remain green or turn bright blue rather than tan. They also are smaller and easier to feed.*

are not so large they cannot be handled, seldom become aggressive, and are not diet specialists, doing well on a largely animal diet with vegetables on the side. The major problems with this beautiful and often very affectionate lizard are that the very young may be delicate and adults need large terraria with enough water in the base to take a swim on occasion. Though they look like Green Iguanas at first glance, they are very different lizards and even belong to a different family (Agamidae rather than Iguanidae).

A typical adult Green Water Dragon is up to 3 feet (90 cm) long, with a large head, very large eyes, a strong spiny crest on the nape and middle of the back, and a long, strong tail that is flattened from side to side and crested above. The hind legs are very long and carry long, wide toes that aid the lizard in swimming. In its natural range in Southeast Asia (including southern China), Green Water Dragons are found along tropical forest streams and lakes, living in trees and escaping to the water when disturbed. Their terrarium must always contain a water basin that is at least as long as the lizard and deep enough to let it soak and even swim. Without this plus mistings several times a day, a Green Water Dragon will dehydrate and die. They also need warm conditions, between 80 and 85F (27 and 30C), never dropping below 60F (16C); these temperatures must be maintained all year. A basking light over a favorite branch and full-spectrum lighting (along with occasional basking in the sun during the warm days of summer) also are essential. The bottom of the terrarium can be covered with a good grade of hardwood reptile bedding; a variety of branches and real or artificial plants is necessary as well. An adult Green Water Dragon needs a terrarium at least 48 inches (122 cm) long and proportionately high to not be stressed. These cage requirements may be too much for the average casual hobbyist, so consider carefully before deciding on one of these lizards as a pet.

Feeding is easy, at least with adults. Provide a diet that is two-thirds animal protein (crickets, mealworms, waxworms, other insects, and especially pinkie mice) and one-third plants (chopped kale, squash, carrots, collard greens, some fruit, etc.). Young specimens need substantial vitamin and calcium supplementation; make sure they start eating pinkie mice as soon as possible to make later feeding easier. Hatchlings often are very delicate for the first six months, but if they make it to a year they usually do well thereafter. Breeding is complicated because of the large size and aquatic needs of the adults.

As captive-bred Green Water Dragons become more common (never purchase wild-collected specimens, which do very poorly in captivity) their popularity is sure to increase. Juveniles may be nervous and flighty, bumping into cage walls, but adults that have been properly handled are gentle, tame pets that get along well with humans and other Green Water Dragons. Perhaps some day they will totally replace the Green Iguana in the pet market, but until then the patient hobbyist able to give them the cage conditions they need couldn't ask for a better pet.

Your first Green Water Dragon should be captive-bred and not so young that it is nervous and difficult to feed. Wild-caught dragons are difficult to acclimate. Because of cage requirements, Green Water Dragons may be hard for the average keeper to house.

The Best Turtles

Frankly, I am of the opinion that at the moment there is no species of turtle or tortoise that makes a truly satisfactory pet for beginners and casual keepers. There are only some 300 species of turtles to choose from to start, a tenth or less of the number of lizards and snakes available, so pickings are slim at best. Add to this the fact that very few turtles are bred in captivity in commercial numbers, plus a general tendency for more and more areas to legislate against owning many or all species of turtles, and you have a real problem. The old standard turtle pets, especially the Red-eared Slider, *Trachemys scripta elegans,* though often bred in captivity on turtle farms, now cannot be legally shipped across state lines in the U.S. as hatchlings because of the threat of salmonellosis infections. They also are unwelcome in many parts of Europe because of competition between the sliders and native turtles when sliders are released into the wild by unthinking hobbyists. Even the tortoises are problematic species, with few truly adaptable to indoor conditions in many parts of the world and many threatened in their home countries. Recently interstate Leopard Tortoise movements have been restricted, probably on a temporary basis, in the U.S. because they may be imported carrying ticks that are the host of a potentially serious cattle disease.

The following thus is my rather grudging listing of "best" pet turtles. All should be taken with a grain of salt as truly adaptable pets, and perhaps none should be recommended for casual keepers:

1) Red-footed Tortoise
2) Stinkpot or Common Musk Turtle
3) Painted Turtle
4) Eastern Box Turtle
5) Leopard Tortoise.

One: Red-footed Tortoise (*Geochelone carbonaria*)

Native to much of tropical America from eastern Panama to northern Argentina, this is a large (adults commonly are 12 to 18 inches, 30 to 46 cm, long) and heavy species with a low-domed carapace and bright red or orange spots on the head and legs in average specimens. Cleanly marked specimens usually have a small, sharply defined yellow spot on each scute of the carapace against a dark brown (often almost black) background. This pretty tortoise is one of the few species that tolerates considerable variation in humidity and temperature, though it is not happy below 70F (21C) or in dry climates. Like all tortoises, they do best when kept outdoors during the warmer days of the year, grazing peacefully on grasses and other low plants and accepting salads of chopped mixed greens (collard, kale, carrot tops, endive, etc.) and some fruit. Adults also will take some animal protein such as catfood, but this must be offered only in very small quantities as a treat to prevent kidney damage and malformed growth; animal protein should not be fed to juveniles. Their preferred temperature range is between 75 and 85F (24 and 30C), and they like warm showers and heavy mistings to maintain humidity. In captive indoor conditions they require a large

Red-footed Tortoises, Geochelone carbonaria, *may be one of the few tortoises that can be safely kept indoors and are moderately adaptable to somewhat cool climates, but they always do best if kept outdoors during the heat of summer.*

The "pyramids" on the shell of this Red-foot may be due to too much animal protein in the diet or lack of sufficient sunlight. Red-foots prefer warm, humid conditions.

run with low sides, full-spectrum fluorescent lights, and one or two basking lights over preferred areas in which to build their body core temperature to active levels. A soft bedding material that stays moist but not wet should form a thick layer in the bottom, and there must be a large water bath available. Keep the cage clean and feed only fresh salads and a good grade of suitable commercial tortoise food.

Red-footed Tortoises are bred in fair numbers, and captive-bred specimens are available though far from inexpensive. These tortoises grow faster than most, reaching maturity in just four years if kept well (preferably outdoors in summer). Males recognize females by sight and scent and engage in a courtship that consists of following the female and butting her shell with theirs. An average female may lay two dozen eggs a year in two clutches, these hatching in four to six months when incubated at 80 to 86F (27 to 30C) in moist vermiculite.

Hatchlings are only 2 inches (5 cm) long and may be very colorful, with the yellow spots covering most of each carapace scute and often with reddish accents strongly developed. They are delicate and not easy to raise, being subject to respiratory ills from drafts, dry weather, and temperatures that drop below 60F (16C) for even a few hours.

Because of their adaptability, half-grown (two years old) to adult captive-bred Red-footed Tortoises are hardy enough to survive well in many marginal situations such as are likely to be found in captivity. They definitely do best when kept outdoors for at least four months each year, but can be grown to adulthood indoors with care.

Almost as adaptable is the very similar, hard to distinguish, Yellow-footed Tortoise, *Geochelone denticulata,* which reaches 30 inches (76 cm) in length and perhaps 100 pounds (45 kilos) in weight. Hatchling Red-foots have a smooth anterior edge to the carapace (behind the head), while in Yellow-foots there are several strong denticles at the edges of the anterior scutes. Never purchase a hatchling of either species or a wild-collected specimen.

Two: Stinkpot or Common Musk Turtle *(Sternotherus odoratus)*

What it lacks in color, the Stinkpot makes up for in character and hardiness. This small (seldom over 5 inches, 12.5 cm, in length) blackish brown aquatic turtle can be found from southeastern Canada south to Florida and central Texas and may be active almost any month of the year. Though a few specimens are captive-bred as a by-product of southern turtle farms, most specimens seen are self-collected or traded; like other turtles under 4 inches (10 cm) in length, it cannot be shipped commercially across state lines in the U.S. because of a fear it could carry salmonellosis. In color this is an undistinguished turtle, the shell being dark blackish brown, as is the skin. There are two narrow yellow-white stripes on each side of the head, running from the snout onto the neck; the plastron (lower shell) usually is pale with dark mottling, and adults have a weak hinge across the plastron that is barely movable. Hatchlings are a bit more colorful, black with a large white spot on each scute, especially the marginals (at the edge of the shell); they also have a strong middorsal keel and a weaker keel on each side of the shell. With growth the keels weaken and finally become almost invisible, the center of the shell actually becoming depressed in old adults. The snout is sharply pointed and the feet are strongly webbed, with sharp claws.

Stinkpots, which get both their common names from a mildly smelly substance secreted through small pores in the bridges between the upper and lower shells, are superbly adapted to walking on the bottom of shallow, often muddy, waters, sticking their snout into the debris of the bottom in search of food. They eat literally anything, from insects and snails to algae and carrion. Captives are fond of small bits of meaty foods as well as earthworms and tubifex worms, and they also rip through elodea and other soft aquatic plants. Stinkpots are active and can digest food at temperatures between about 60 and 85F (16 and 30C), becoming stressed at temperatures much over 90F (32C). They tolerate cold well, becoming inactive in debris on the bottom, but cease to feed and grow.

Because shallow waters become cold or hot much faster than deeper waters and also become fouled or silted readily, Stinkpots adapt well to almost any keeping conditions. They live well in aquaria with filtration (they produce relatively little waste compared to most other aquatic turtles), as long as they are allowed to reach the surface to breathe. They climb very well and can escape from uncovered tanks by climbing up branches or even the glue at the corners, so anchor tops securely. Stinkpots seldom bask as such, so they do not need a basking light, though exposure to sunlight occasionally or to fluorescent lights doesn't hurt.

They are even easier to keep as single specimens in small (5-gallon, 19-L), unfiltered plastic tanks (lighter than glass and easier to handle) with just enough water in the bottom to cover the turtle. Food is placed in a corner and the water is changed and the tank cleaned every two or three days at most. Since Stinkpots don't need special heating to grow in the average household, such a simple tank can be placed in front of a window receiving weak sunlight for a few hours a day to keep water temperatures up and give the turtle some exposure to UV light. Since Stinkpots dehydrate rapidly, they should never be left out of water or at least moist paper towels more than an hour or two.

These little turtles breed through much of the year, especially in the South, a female producing two or three clutches of three to five eggs each. The eggs often are barely covered with soil and may be laid under logs or litter just a little distance from the water. The eggs hatch in 80 days or so, with most young emerging in late summer to early autumn. With luck, a hatchling will not be eaten by the numerous fishes, snakes, birds, and mammals that prey on them (perhaps 80% of any clutch will be eaten in their first year) and will reach sexual maturity by the age of three or four (males) or four to nine (females) years. These are very long-lived turtles if they reach adulthood, females commonly living over 20 years, with one record of 54 years.

Stinkpots have a nice personality and don't mind being handled, though they do bite and scratch if in a bad mood or disturbed suddenly. They have a very large mouth with sharp beaks, but their bite is easy to avoid. They are not shy turtles and don't hide or try to escape (unless allowed to climb out). Their hardiness makes them an excellent choice in a pet, and they really are difficult to kill or mistreat without special malice. Of all the turtles in this "best" pet list, the Stinkpot is certainly the hardiest.

Equally hardy but larger and thus more complicated to keep are other species of *Sternotherus* (especially the Keeled Musk Turtle, *Sternotherus carinatus*, of the Deep South) and the closely related *Kinosternon* (mud turtles), some of which are imports from tropical America and have interesting head patterns and colors.

If you want a personable little turtle that is easy to care for and inexpensive, the Stinkpot, Sternotherus odoratus, *may be just your cup of tea. However, even it requires regular maintenance.*

Three: Painted Turtle (*Chrysemys picta*)

Though many aquatic turtles are sold for hobbyists, with hatchlings often peddled very cheaply for children, these turtles usually are poor choices as pets. In addition to almost all young aquatic turtles carrying the bacteria that cause salmonellosis (which rarely may be fatal to children and adults with impaired health), to successfully maintain an aquatic turtle for many years requires a large aquarium with an expensive filtering unit that will keep the water clean and odor-free. Freshwater turtles are notorious for being dirty feeders, excreting large amounts of waste that, because it usually contains fish, also is oily and difficult to clean. A partial exception to this is the small Painted Turtle, a widespread and abundant native of the eastern and central U.S. and southern Canada. Painted Turtles are relatively flat-shelled, with greenish brown to nearly black carapaces that bear yellow lines along the seams of the scutes and red spots on the marginals. The bridges and plastron usually are red and yellow with black markings, and there are red and yellow lines on the legs and neck. Details of pattern vary with the several subspecies, but all Paints are very pretty turtles. Large adult females may be 6 inches (15 cm) long, but males seldom exceed 4 inches (10 cm), helping make this species more suitable to terrarium conditions than most other aquatics.

Paints are strong baskers, spending several hours a day during the spring to autumn exposed to the sunlight in order to reach a body core temperature of over 75F (24C), at which they can digest food. They eat almost anything, from small crayfishes, shrimp, and insects to aquatic plants and carrion. Juveniles take mostly animal protein, adding plants to the diet after their first year. Like other freshwater turtles, they produce a lot of waste and need to be kept in a heavily filtered aquarium, but their small adult size makes it possible to keep one or two specimens in a 20-gallon (76-L) aquarium. Use a heater to keep the water temperature at 80F (27C), and provide a basking light plus full-spectrum fluorescent lights to allow the turtle to bask as normal. If the shell begins to get spotty or corroded, the water is too dirty. Painted Turtles can survive (though not feed) at very low temperatures, so if you have difficulties maintaining a set temperature, err to the lower levels.

Because few Painted Turtles, especially males, exceed the 4-inch (10-cm) minimum required for interstate shipment of turtles in the U.S., Paints are not widely sold, but they are easy to collect or obtain in trade. A few, especially of the southern subspecies with a red stripe down the center of the back, are captive-bred at turtle farms in the southern U.S., so it is possible to obtain pets that have never been in the wild. Though a challenge, many hobbyists have had excellent luck keeping Paints, among the most beautiful of the North American turtles.

Four: Eastern Box Turtle (*Terrapene carolina*)

Listing this common box turtle as a "best" pet is sure to draw criticism from some readers. Though they have a long history as pets and are widely available at low cost in many areas, American box turtles (two species, the Eastern and the Ornate or Western, *Terrapene ornata*, are commonly kept, with other rarely seen species coming from Mexico) are slow to mature and produce only a few young each year, so though long-lived they are very subject to collecting pressure and loss of habitat. Box turtles often adapt well to human company, feeding in yards and gardens, though they are killed in horrendous numbers on the roads, but they cannot cope with mass col-

Painted Turtles, Chrysemys picta, *occur across the U.S. and southern Canada in the form of several subspecies; this is* belli, *found from Missouri to the Pacific Northwest. All the subspecies have much the same keeping requirements.*

lecting techniques used to supply animals to commercial markets. For these reasons, only captive-bred box turtles, either Eastern or Ornate, can be given any recommendation as pets. Wild-caught specimens must not be purchased if you care about the future of the species. Be aware that some dealers sell near-hatchlings and other very young box turtles as though captive-bred when they are really wild-collected; you should see some type of proof of captive origin. Keepers around the country maintain large groups of box turtles in outdoor settings, where they breed freely, producing sometimes dozens of young each year. If you look around, such captive-breds are available and are not expensive. Unfortunately, some areas have totally prohibited the keeping of box turtles (some or all species) on the basis that the turtles are threatened locally and it is not possible to tell imports from local specimens. Know all your local laws before obtaining a box turtle, even if you find one locally and rescue it from certain death on the highway.

Once you get around these political and ecological problems, you face a greater problem with box turtles: they almost have to be kept outdoors from late spring through early autumn to remain healthy, and they also do best in the area where they were hatched. If you do not have a suitably escape-proof garden with suitable plants and shelter, you will have great difficulty keeping a box turtle.

The Eastern Box Turtle has a wide range over much of the eastern U.S. west to central Texas (the Ornate Box Turtle is resident from the Great Plains into southern Arizona in drier habitats) in open and wooded habitats, often near water but sometimes in very dry pinelands. Though often thought of as a tortoise, they actually are close relatives of the sliders and cooters, fully aquatic American turtles, and can swim well and often overwinter under the mud of a lake or stream. Typical Eastern Box Turtles are 5 to 8 inches (12.5 to 20 cm) long, with a strongly domed carapace and a plastron (lower shell) with a strong hinge across the front center of the shell. There is a tremendous amount of variation, some individual, some geographic, in shape and coloration, and scientists often recognize four subspecies. They range from dull brown over the carapace and skin of the head and legs to brown with brilliant yellow and orange spots and blotches over the entire carapace plus bright red, yellow, and orange spots and blotches on the head and legs. The pale pattern on the carapace may be absent, fine spotting, irregular blotches, or narrow radiating lines. Specimens of almost any coloration and pattern can be found almost anywhere in the range, so identification of subspecies must be based on a true scientific study of a long series of specimens or on known collecting localities. The most brightly colored specimens often are the small southern three-toed (on the hind foot) subspecies *T. c. triunguis.*

They may vary in color, but Eastern Box Turtles are all similar in their requirements, being omnivores active from the end of freezing weather to the first frosts of autumn. They take insects, snails, carrion, earthworms, small fishes (in aquatic situations), mushrooms, fruits of all kinds, and softer greens. They even have been seen eating small snakes, frogs, and birds (probably dead before ingestion) and chew on mammal bones as a source of calcium. In a garden they search for worms and insects and also feed on dandelions, roses, and other common plants, plus sometimes grasses. Their natural diet should be supplemented with a variety of animal and plant foods as well as a bit of catfood on occasion, plus extra vitamins and calcium every other week. Captives often will not feed on plants that are not familiar to them, so it is easier to maintain a specimen in the area in which it grew up. Like other terrestrial turtles, they usually emerge in the morning to find a sunny spot and bask in the sunlight to warm up, feeding once they are warm enough and then retreating when the sun becomes too warm. They feed again in the late afternoon before retiring for the evening to a protected area that is used night after night. With the coming of cool weather in the autumn, they bury themselves under leaves, soil, and debris, sometimes in the water, and go far enough down to avoid frozen ground.

Mating occurs in the spring, males searching for and following females often for long periods before going through special head-bobbing and leg movements and mounting for copulation. A gravid female digs a nest in which to lay four or five eggs (often fewer) that hatch in some three months, young emerging just before it is time to look for cover for the winter. A female may lay several clutches a year and can produce fertile eggs for up to four years after a single mating. Hatchlings are relatively flat, brown turtles with large yellow knobs down the center of the back and yellow spots on each scute. They grow slowly because they seldom can feed heavily before the following spring and seldom are sexually mature until they are five to eight years old. Eastern Box Turtles are famous for their longevity, with at least a few individuals reaching a century and many seeming to live 20 to 50 years.

Kept outdoors in a suitably large yard or garden with an escape-proof fence, protected areas such as leaf piles in which to overwinter, and access to sunny basking spots, Eastern Box Turtles may be easy to keep and excellent pets that will reproduce regularly. Their diet should always be supplemented with a wider variety of foods than available naturally to them, and they must be protected from predators such as dogs and cats, birds, and invading raccoons and opossums. Allow the turtles to follow a natural seasonal rhythm. A problem to be considered is that Eastern Box Turtles originating in the South may not have innate instincts to burrow deeply enough to avoid freezing during northern winters, and thus may die in the winter. Similarly, turtles of northern origin may stop feeding too early when kept in the South and may attempt to escape a winter that never occurs, again dying during the winter. If possible, try to obtain animals captive-bred in the area where they will be kept as adults.

If kept indoors, Eastern Box Turtles are more complicated charges as they must be provided with heat from below, basking lights from above, and full-spectrum fluorescent lights to provide sufficient UV light for satisfactory shell formation. They also may die of stress if not allowed to go through their natural overwintering rest period, so they must be removed to a cool storage area during the winter. Keeping an Eastern Box Turtle (or any other box turtle, for that matter) indoors probably is too difficult for the casual hobbyist.

Somewhat similar in appearance and behavior to the American box turtles are the unrelated Asian box turtles of the genus *Cuora*. Several species are available, almost always as wild-caught imports that may be severely stressed and parasitized. Some of the species are fully aquatic turtles, while even the more terrestrial species still are strongly associated with water. Once vetted and given a habitat suitable for the species, some individuals survive to make excellent pets, but most

If legally keepable in your area, and if you have access to outdoor runs, Eastern Box Turtles, Terrapene carolina, make good turtle pets. However, few hobbyists have both these factors going for them.

Ornate Box Turtles, Terrapene ornata, *are just as keepable as Eastern Boxes, but they have exactly the same problems. Captive-bred specimens of both species are difficult to find but are available for the persistent hobbyist.*

will die in a few weeks or months after importation. Additionally, all the species of this genus are being subjected to massive collecting throughout southern Asia to supply native food and medicinals markets in China and other countries, and some species that once were common may now be rapidly disappearing from all or parts of their range. Until captive-bred specimens are readily available, and until more is known about the actual requirements for each species, these attractive turtles are best avoided by the casual keeper.

Five: Leopard Tortoise (*Geochelone pardalis*)

With adults 12 to 18 inches (30 to 46 cm) long and a strikingly high-domed profile, the Leopard Tortoise is one of the most beautiful of its group. Widely distributed over dry savannas and similar habitats from the Sudan to South Africa, this is a variable tortoise that generally is very pale brown to ivory with many irregular black or dark brown specks and spots scattered over the carapace, especially near the seams of the scutes. This spotted pattern develops with growth from a much more simple and colorful juvenile pattern of irregular concentric black circles around a reddish brown center on each scute. Sometimes very old, large individuals may be mostly brown, much like a very high-domed Sulcata (*Geochelone sulcata*).

These tortoises like warm, dry climates and do not survive well in the cooler, more humid climate of much of the U.S. and Europe. They thrive in southern California and parts of Arizona, and there are indications that captive-bred specimens may have become a bit more adaptable to higher humidities than their ancestors. However, specimens raised indoors or outdoors in much of the eastern U.S. are likely to develop distorted shells marked by conical scutes that serve to help increase lung capacity. Such distortions also may occur from feeding animal protein to young, actively growing specimens, so avoid catfood even as a treat for youngsters. Catfood and other animal proteins may damage the kidneys as well.

Kept outdoors during the summer and provided with a heated shed in which to get out of the evening cold or drafts, Leopard Tortoises feed on a variety of grasses and other low plants and also on salads of chopped greens and fruits. Kept indoors, they need a room to themselves or at least a run that is heavily lighted with full-spectrum fluorescents and has several basking lights. As usual, never start with a delicate hatchling (unfortunately the least expensive specimens to purchase) but instead buy a specimen at least two years old and without obvious malformations of the shell. Because of their size, these tortoises are difficult for the non-specialist to breed, but females lay 10 to 20 eggs in a clutch. The eggs may take as long as eight months to hatch.

If you live in a suitable climate, with relatively low humidity and warm winters, a Leopard Tortoise may just do well for you, but it would be best to consult local keepers first to get more information on the regional situation. Though widely available as captive-breds and sold as a beginner's tortoise, keeping a Leopard in improper conditions may be a death sentence.

This young Leopard Tortoise, Geochelone pardalis, *has not yet acquired the adult spotted pattern. Leopards are very subject to deformed shells from high humidity surroundings and animal protein in the diet.*

A Few Reptiles
to Avoid

The following reptiles are not necessarily bad pets or unkeepable, but they just are too much for an inexperienced or beginning hobbyist to take on as a responsibility. All these reptiles have their fans, and many are captive-bred in good numbers each year, making them inexpensive and readily available. For reasons that should become obvious, they require more patience or skill in keeping than do the "best" reptile species talked about earlier.

Giant Pythons and Anacondas

Baby Burmese Pythons (*Python molurus bivittatus*), Reticulated Pythons (*Python reticulatus*), and both Green and Yellow Anacondas (*Eunectes murinus* and *E. notaeus*, respectively) are widely available at reptile shows across the U.S. and in Europe, and sometimes they even are sold in pet shops. These captive-bred babies generally are some 2 feet (0.6 meter) long, often very gentle, and may have brilliant color patterns. Thought of in the same terms as colubrid snakes, they should make excellent pets. Additionally, they often are very inexpensive.

Unfortunately, these snakes all grow rapidly and in two to three years will be some 12 feet (3.6 meters) long and often weigh well over 50 pounds (22.5 kilos). Additionally, they are feeding machines that require expensive foods such as large rats and rabbits by this age and they also can push apart almost any common terrarium. In another year or two they will require two or three people in attendance each time they are handled, and adults of both Burmese and Reticulated Pythons have killed adult keepers. Both the Burmese Python and the Reticulated Python often exceed 20 feet (6 meters) in captivity. The anacondas are a bit smaller and slower-growing than the pythons, but they are even more massive animals that require large swimming pools for their comfort and good health. All these snakes can inflict serious bites capable of permanently damaging deep muscles, nerves, and blood vessels.

If you must have a giant snake, be sure you can provide it with a room of its own, because you cannot let it have the run of the house (other pets and small children are both potential prey). Adequately feeding a giant snake is very expensive, as is every aspect of its care. The albino Burmese Python is one of the most attractive of all the snakes and is bred in very large numbers (some say too large numbers) each year, so it is the giant most often seen for sale. Adult Burmese Pythons are relatively even-tempered for a giant snake, but they remain unpredictable; any accident could be serious, painful, expensive, and possibly even terminal. Yellow Anacondas are smaller than the other species mentioned, seldom exceeding 12 feet (3.6 meters) in length, and are less aquatic than the Green Anaconda, but they still are massive snakes that require a large swimming area for comfort. The bite from an anaconda is very painful and often transmits bacteria and amoebae that may cause systemic infections that are difficult to control even with the proper antibiotics and other injectibles.

These snakes will exceed 8 to 12 feet (2.4 to 3.6 meters) in length by the time they are 24 months old, which means that they will then be illegal to own in private households in areas where dangerous animal laws are in effect. Such laws usually set maximum lengths of between 8 and 10 feet (2.4 and 3 meters) for snakes kept as pets. Dangerous animal laws are becoming more common across the world and are being enforced in many areas. Zoos seldom will take displaced giant snakes, and some desperate owners have resorted to just releasing their former pets into local parks, leading to disasters for all concerned.

Until you have the experience and the facilities for keeping giant snakes, just enjoy looking at them but do not buy them.

Giant Green Iguanas

The Giant Green Iguana (*Iguana iguana*) is perhaps the most commonly sold and widely seen pet reptile, but this does not mean that it makes a suitable pet for most households. This very large (often over 5 feet, 1.5 meters, long from snout to tip of tail), large-clawed arboreal (tree-climbing) lizard ranges from Mexico to central South America and has adapted to a variety of habitats from rain forest to near desert, and it does adapt well to captivity—but needs special care. Three major problems combine to make Giant Green Iguanas unsuitable as pets for beginning hobbyists.

First is the source of the specimens. As of today, almost all of the baby Green Iguanas sold in shops are the result of farming programs in a few Central and South American countries. Wild gravid females are collected and held until they lay their eggs or a brood stock of several wild-collected adult pairs is maintained much like cattle. The eggs are collected, incubated in the country of origin, and hatchlings are shipped to the United States and other markets in tremendous numbers (perhaps as many as a million young a year). They are not captive-bred in a strict sense, as the matings are not controlled and the young are not accustomed to human handling before sale. Many young Green Iguanas suffer from respiratory ills and severe stress from shipment in very confined conditions, and many die a few months after reaching the market.

Second is the diet problem. In nature Green Iguanas feed almost exclusively on leaves of trees and shrubs, almost all of species that are not grown in temperate climates. They occasionally take some fruit, and young specimens may take an occasional insect or two. These lizards have very narrow diet requirements that must be met or they will die. The diet in captivity usually consists of a salad of a wide variety of green leafy vegetables, a bit of fruit, and vitamin and calcium supplements. Green Iguanas have high calcium requirements that must be met, especially in young, fast-growing individuals, or they will suffer and die.

Thirdly, these are big, active animals quite able to defend themselves against large predators, including humans. An adult male Green Iguana may be 6 feet (1.8 meters) long, about half of this muscular tail. A slap from the tail can break the skin; all four feet have large, sharply-pointed claws that can wreak havoc on human bodies as well as furniture; and the teeth, though adapted for cutting and chewing leaves, are arrowhead-shaped and have serrated edges that can inflict deep, serious wounds. Additionally, males in rutting condition have been known to attack female keepers; they may be aggressive for several months each year. Their large size means very large cages, while their tropical origin requires strong basking lights and a background temperature that seldom drops below 80F (27C) even during the winter.

Giant Green Iguanas may make very personable pets, and some keepers seem to have a natural knack for keeping these lizards. However, for the beginner or a keeper with limited time and resources these lizards cannot be recommended.

Venomous Snakes and Beaded Lizards

Some of the most beautiful snakes are venomous—these include many Gaboon Vipers and relatives (genus *Bitis*), a multitude of tropical tree and palm vipers (*Bothrops, Trimeresurus, Tropidolaemus,* and *Atheris,* among others), and the North American Copperheads (*Agkistrodon contortrix*) and many rattlesnakes (*Crotalus*). Only two lizards, the Gila Monster (*Heloderma suspectum*) and the Mexican

Juvenile Burmese Pythons, Python molurus bivittatus, *are beautiful snakes and easily affordable, but this species grows too fast and too large for keeping in the average household.*

Beaded Lizard (*Heloderma horridum*), are venomous, and both are kept and bred by advanced hobbyists. Ardent fanciers of these animals tend to downplay the dangers of these snakes and lizards, and it is not uncommon to hear that some palm viper has a bite "no more dangerous than a bee sting." Unfortunately, this just is not true. From hatching or birth to death, all the vipers (family Viperidae) are dangerously venomous, and almost every species that has been kept has caused serious bites on occasion, with deaths not uncommon. (In the United States, for the last several decades almost all deaths from venomous snake bites have resulted from the snake being handled by the victim, often under captive conditions.) Even the relatively small and gorgeously colored Eyelash and Temple Vipers (*Bothrops schlegeli* and *Tropidolaemus wagleri,* respectively) can produce bites that will result in several days of hospitalization and enormous medical bills, along with scarring and often permanent damage to a hand or foot. The bite from even a small Gaboon Viper (*Bitis gabonicus*) is enough to kill an adult human, a consequence that has happened several times in the United States.

In the United States and Europe most areas require special permits before a venomous snake can be kept as a pet. The permits are difficult to get, often require the posting of large monetary bonds, and may make demands on how cages are to be constructed and maintained. Average hobbyists seldom can obtain such permits, which probably is to the good. Antivenin may have to be stocked or confirmed as available at a cooperating hospital or zoo; antivenin is expensive and has a relatively short shelf-life, as well as requiring medical testing before it can be safely administered. The bite from even a relatively "safe" venomous snake may require several vials of antivenin for treatment, at a horrendous cost.

Perhaps not surprisingly, some hobbyists keep cobras and their relatives (family Elapidae), especially some of the colorful species of *Aspidelaps*. The same problems apply to keeping these snakes as with the vipers, but perhaps more so. Cobras (*Naja, Ophiophagus, Haemachatus*) are without exception deadly snakes where even a casual bite may result in death. The smaller elapids are variable in their toxicity, but none regularly available can be considered harmless and some are surprisingly toxic relative to their small size.

Unless you have a real reason to keep a venomous snake, these animals are best avoided as pets. If you must keep one, be sure you comply with all requirements, legal and logical, and try to talk with several advanced keepers before you become involved with these incredible snakes.

Caimans and Alligators

Occasionally you will see very young Spectacled Caimans (*Caiman crocodilus*) or even American Alligators (*Alligator mississippiensis*) offered for sale at reptile shows or even in pet shops. Few reptiles are more appealing than a young crocodilian, but few reptiles are less keepable by the average hobbyist. No crocodilian is less than 4 feet (1.2 meters) long when adult, much of this a muscular tail and a long, tooth-laden snout. These all are dangerous animals when adult—make no mistake, that baby caiman will soon become an incredibly strong, often very aggressive monster.

Adult caimans and alligators are difficult to confine because of their size, which eliminates most commercially available aquaria, and their strength, which allows them to simply push apart any ordinary construction. Often they are given their own room and a wading pool. Both the Spectacled Caiman and the American Alligator commonly exceed 6 feet (1.8 meters) in length and have a mouth

Juvenile American Alligators, Alligator mississippiensis, *recently have become legally salable again, but many areas have laws against keeping any crocodilian. Remember what the pretty babies will grow into in just a few years—these are not suitable pets.*

easily able to engulf an entire hand. They also are dirty animals to keep, feeding mostly on oily fishes in captivity, and maintenance of such a large, dangerous animal is a risky chore.

Crocodiles (*Crocodylus*) are even worse pets than caimans and alligators, often being more massive and much more aggressive even as hatchlings. I honestly cannot think of any reason for a hobbyist who keeps reptiles in a family home to possess any crocodilian.

Assorted Tortoises

Some tortoises make excellent pets, and the Red-foot even ranks first on my "best" list. However, others are almost impossible to keep successfully. These include the several species of *Testudo* from the Mediterranean area and southwestern Asia. Though attractive and once widely available, they make poor pets because they cannot adjust to climates in much of the United States and Europe. Cool, moist weather rapidly leads to death, so outside their home areas they are most keepable only in southern California and the American Southwest, areas with a relatively dry, so-called Mediterranean climate. They also have extremely high calcium demands that are difficult to meet if they are kept indoors under controlled climatic conditions. Fortunately, almost all the *Testudo* species now are protected by various national and international laws and are no longer easy to obtain unless you have enough experience to qualify for the proper permits.

Legal restrictions also mean that most other tortoises are no longer easy to get, and because so few are really keepable, this probably is for the best. The gopher tortoises (*Gopherus*) of the southern

United States and northern Mexico, for instance, are losing habitat to human development, are dying from introduced respiratory diseases, and almost never adapt to captive keeping outside the area in which they were hatched. That they are no longer available commercially is for the best, as it holds out the possibility that these tortoises will continue to be watchable in nature. The legal status of all tortoises from Madagascar, southern Africa, and India is in doubt—if you must have a specimen from one of these areas, be sure you have perfect documentation showing their legal importation or origin from legally obtained parents.

For that matter, few tortoises are widely captive-bred. One exception, the African Spurred Tortoise or Sulcata (*Geochelone sulcata*), is widely available but probably should be avoided by beginners and non-specialists. Sulcatas often are over 30 inches (76 cm) long and may weigh well over 100 pounds (45 kilos). They are digging machines that have been known to tunnel under garages and outbuildings, causing the buildings to collapse. They need constant dry conditions at temperatures between 80 and almost 90F (27 and 32C), so they require special outdoor accommodations at all times. Such large tortoises have gigantic appetites and produce an equivalent amount of waste, so maintenance is no simple chore. Recently, escaped Sulcatas have caused headline stories in the newspapers and on television, helping give all reptile keeping a bad reputation. *Geochelone sulcata*, though easily available as captive-breds, just is too large for its own good under most circumstances.

Others

With almost 8,000 reptile species theoretically available to hobbyists, it is impossible to predict what could become available in any particular shop at any particular time. As a general rule, do not purchase any animal that cannot be identified to species with confidence. If you do not know the identity of a reptile, you cannot find the correct information on where it came from (commercial importation sources often are secret) and how best to attempt to keep it. Avoid any snake or lizard that has unusual or very narrow dietary requirements. Many attractive snakes, for instance, feed on small skinks, anoles, and other lizards or on small frogs. Though these food animals may be abundant in tropical forests, they are difficult or impossible to culture and will not be available all year to the average hobbyist. This means that a lizard- or frog-specialist must either be hibernated when food is unavailable (and many tropical snakes do not hibernate) or face the risks of a prolonged involuntary non-feeding period. Lack of suitable foods usually means death in a few months. Many smaller snakes and arboreal (tree-dwelling) tropical species feed on snails and slugs, which may be impossible to substitute with locally available species. If you don't know anything about a reptile, don't buy it.

Even some species that are widely available are actually too delicate to be kept by the average hobbyist. Rough Green Snakes (*Opheodrys aestivus*), for instance, though found widely over the southeastern United States and regularly collected for the terrarium, are delicate charges in the terrarium and often will not feed. The problem may be that mostly adults are collected and shipped for the hobby, and these are adapted to feeding on a variety of small caterpillars and other insects that the hobbyist cannot duplicate. Captive-bred specimens are almost unavailable, but these do much better in captivity, taking crickets and waxworms.

If possible, always buy captive-bred specimens of ANY reptile you want to keep as a pet.

Index

Page numbers in **bold** represent photographs

Index

Photo Credits

Randall D. Babb: 54
Marian Bacon: 4 (Physignathus cocincinus); 9; 56 (Iguana iguana)
R. D. Bartlett: 15 (top & bottom); 24; 31; 36; 37; 41; 44 (Terrapene carolina); 51
Allen Both: 33; 59
Suzanne L. Collins: 53
Isabelle Francais: 17
Paul Freed: 14
James E. Gerholdt: 47; 61
Eric Loza: 6; 13; 20
Sean McKeown: 39
Gerold & Cindy Merker: 1 (Elaphe guttata); 8; 10 (Elaphe guttata); 19; 21; 23; 26 (Eublepharis macularius); 29; 34
Aaron Norman: 18; 49; 55
Robert G. Sprackland: 42
Karl H. Switak: 7; 22; 43; 46
John Tyson: 30; 35